Mandalas Coloring Book
Stress Less Coloring Mandalas

Jasmine Andrews

Mandalas Coloring Book
Stress Less Coloring Mandalas

ISBN-13: 978-1542737562

ISBN-10: 1542737567

Thank you

www.ingramcontent.com/pod-product-compliance
Lightning Source LLC
Chambersburg PA
CBHW081125180526
45170CB00008B/3017
* 9 7 8 1 5 4 2 7 3 7 5 6 2 *